This book belongs to

_____

From

_____

Message

_____

_____

_____

_____

Dedicated to: Little Thomas, Philippe and to all the other children.

Original title of the book: *Il nuovo libro del decoupage*

© Edizioni GRIBAUDO Srl
Via Natale Battaglia, 12 – Milano
www.edizionigribaudo.it

Text adapted by Serena Dei
Illustrations by Chiara Raineri
Bible advisor: Father Martino Signoretto

Copyright © 2012 by Christian Art Kids, an imprint of Christian Art Publishers,
PO Box 1599, Vereeniging, 1930, RSA

359 Longview Drive, Bloomingdale, IL 60108, USA

First edition 2012

Translated from the French edition by Etienne le Roux

Printed in China

ISBN 978-1-4321-0039-1

12 13 14 15 16 17 18 19 20 21 – 10 9 8 7 6 5 4 3 2 1

Best-Loved
Bible Stories
for Children

Illustrations by Chiara Raineri

CONTENTS

THE NEW TESTAMENT

The Old Testament

God Creates the World

In the beginning, there was only darkness. God said, "Let there be light!" And there was light.

Then God separated the sky from the water. He gathered the waters together to make the sea, and dry ground appeared.

During the day the sun shone over all things, and at night the stars and the moon appeared. The changes from light to darkness made it easy to count the days, the weeks, the months and even the years.

Then God made all the fish, big and small, to swim in the sea. He also made the birds to fly in the skies.

Then God made fields and mountains, where the rivers flowed and the grass grew. The flowers smelled very nice and the trees made delicious fruits.

God then decided to put animals on the earth. He made all kinds of animals like dogs, cats, lions, squirrels, frogs, and snakes. He also created ants, spiders, grasshoppers and bees.

God looked at all the animals and He was happy. God then made a man and called him Adam. God took some dust from the ground and shaped it into a man's body. God breathed life into the man. This is how God made Adam. Adam could work the fields, eat fruits from the trees, drink milk from the cows, swim in the sea and play with the dolphins.

God noticed that Adam was alone. God decided to give Adam a friend and called her Eve. God had made everything in six days. On the seventh day He rested.

Adam and Eve

Adam and Eve lived in the Garden of Eden. There were many plants and the animals lived in peace with one another. Adam and Eve were very happy in this garden and they fed themselves with fruits from the trees. There was, however, one tree from which they were not allowed to eat. It was the Tree of the Knowledge of Good and Evil. God had told them, "If you eat only one of its fruits, there will be terrible consequences!"

The devil was also in the garden. He made himself look like a snake. One day he asked Eve, "Did God really say you must not eat the fruit from any of the trees in the garden?" And she answered, "No, God only told us not to eat from the Tree of the Knowledge of Good and Evil."

The snake said, "Taste this fruit, it is delicious.
If you eat it, you will be like God, knowing good and
evil!" Eve tasted the fruit from the forbidden tree and
then gave some to Adam. At that moment, they realized
that they were completely naked and they felt ashamed.

They started to look for leaves to cover themselves.
God knew that Adam and Eve had disobeyed Him.
"Because you have not listened to Me, you must leave
the garden." God was angry and sent them away.
They had to work for their own food.

Cain Kills His Brother Abel

After Adam and Eve ate the fruit from the Tree of the Knowledge of Good and Evil, their lives were never the same again. They knew about good and evil. In order to get their food, they had to fight wild animals and wear animal skins to protect themselves from the cold.

Eve gave birth to two boys. She called the first son Cain and the second son Abel. Cain was a farmer and Abel was a shepherd. One day, Cain and Abel made their sacrifices to the Lord: Abel sacrificed the best lambs of his flock, and Cain offered fruit and vegetables from his garden. The Lord was pleased with the gift from Abel, because He understood the goodness of his heart. But God was not pleased with Cain's offering. Cain was jealous of Abel and left in silence. He was angry with God and hated his brother.

A few days later Cain asked Abel to go out to the field with him. When they were alone, Cain killed his brother and ran away. Then God asked Cain, "Where is your brother?" Cain answered, "How should I know? Am I supposed to look after him?" But God, who knows everything, told Cain to go away, "Leave! You will live far from your family!"

Noah Builds a Big Boat

The earth was filled with Adam and Eve's children and grandchildren. As the years went by, there were more and more people on the earth. The Lord saw that the people on the earth were very bad and that everything they thought about was evil. This made God very sad.

One day, He decided to end all evil and wipe the earth clean with a flood from which only one man and his family would survive. Noah was the only good man on the earth. He had three sons: Shem, Ham and Japheth.

God told Noah, "I am going to send a flood that will destroy everything. But you and your family will be safe in the boat. Bring into the boat a male and female of every kind of animal."

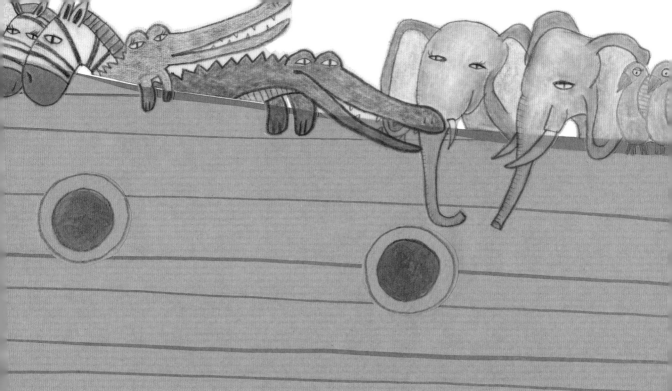

Noah obeyed God. He built a big and very strong boat made of wood. This big boat is also called an ark. Then he gathered everything he would need for the journey. Noah and his family climbed into the boat with the animals. As soon as the last pair was on board, God closed the door and it started to rain. It rained for forty days and forty nights.

It rained and rained. And the water became deeper and deeper until the boat started to float. The water covered the whole earth for a hundred-and-fifty days. During that time, Noah and his family were safe inside the ark.

Then God told the wind to blow, so that the water would dry up and the mountains could be seen. The ark landed on Mount Ararat.

After many days, Noah opened a window from the ark and released a dove. It returned with an olive branch in its beak. This meant that the trees had reappeared, but there was still water covering the earth.

A while later God told Noah that it was time to leave the ark.

Everyone came out of the ark. A new life could now begin on earth.

In the sky, a beautiful rainbow appeared and God told Noah, "This is the sign of the promise between Me and you, and your children after you. I promise never to flood the earth again."

19

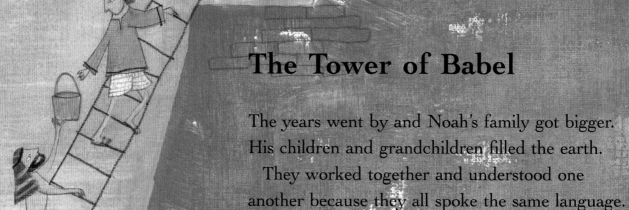

The Tower of Babel

The years went by and Noah's family got bigger.
His children and grandchildren filled the earth.
    They worked together and understood one
another because they all spoke the same language.
They made bricks with fire and built houses.

One day, the people decided to build a city with a tower so high that it could touch the sky! God saw what they were doing and knew that the tower they were building was not proof of the people's love for Him, but rather showed their own pride.

The Lord decided to punish the people by making them speak different languages so that they could not understand one another. They had to stop building the tower. The Lord made them move away from there and they went to live all over the world. That's how the city of Babel got its name.

Abraham and Sarah

Abraham was a descendant of Noah and he lived in the country of Ur.

He was a good man. He was married to a very kind woman named Sarah. Sarah could not have children. One day, the Lord spoke to Abraham and told him, "Leave with your wife and all your belongings and go to a land that I will show you."

Abraham and Sarah did what God asked. When they arrived at their destination, the Lord gave Abraham great news, "Your wife, Sarah, will have a son." Abraham called his son Isaac.

Abraham and Sarah loved little Isaac. A few years later, God decided to test Abraham's faith.

One night, the Lord spoke to Abraham and told him, "Take your son, Isaac, to the top of the mountain and sacrifice him to Me." Poor Abraham was very sad, but obeyed God. When he arrived at the top of the mountain, Abraham told Isaac to collect some wood, explaining that it would be for the sacrifice.

When Isaac had finished, his father laid him down on the wood on the altar.

Then Abraham took his knife and was about to kill his son. But God's angel spoke to him from heaven, "Dear Abraham, you have proven your faith to Me. You and Isaac can go back home and be blessed."

God Finds a Wife for Isaac

Abraham was now a very old man. But before he died, he decided to find a wife for his beloved son, Isaac, who had become a strong and handsome young man. He sent a servant to the place where his brother Nahor lived, to find a kind wife for Isaac.

When the servant arrived at the well near Nahor he stopped with his ten camels. He prayed to the Lord to help him find the right wife for Isaac.

The servant prayed that he would know which girl to choose by asking her for water. If the girl gave him water and also gave his camels water, he would know she was the right one.

Just then Rebekah came to the well. The servant asked her, "May I have some water?" The young lady answered, "Of course! I will give you as much as you want and I will also give water for your camels."

Then he asked her, "Who are you?" She answered, "I am Rebekah, the granddaughter of Nahor." The servant went with Rebekah, and she took him to her father to ask if she could marry Isaac.

When Rebekah's father agreed to the marriage, the young lady and the servant returned to Abraham's home. One evening, Isaac was walking out in the fields and saw the arrival of the beautiful young lady. He immediately fell in love with Rebekah and married her.

Joseph the Dreamer

Isaac and Rebekah had a son named Jacob. Jacob had twelve sons and one daughter.

Jacob loved Joseph more than his other children. Jacob gave him a fancy coat. The other children were very jealous of Joseph.

Joseph told them about a dream he had. The sun, the moon and eleven stars bowed down in front of him. His father asked him if the dream meant that his father, his mother and his brothers had to bow down in front of him. This made Joseph's brothers hate him even more.

Joseph's brothers believed that Joseph saw himself as being better than them. One day Joseph was going to meet his brothers who were looking after the sheep. When they saw Joseph coming they said, "Let's kill him!" But one brother, Reuben, said, "No, let's throw him in this well and tell Father that he has been killed by wild animals."

At the same time, a group of traders were passing by. So the brothers decided to sell Joseph to the traders. They took his beautiful coat and dipped it in blood so that their father would think Joseph had been killed.

The traders took Joseph to Egypt, where they sold him as a slave to Pharaoh's captain of the guards, Potiphar.

The wife of Joseph's new master fell in love with him, but he rejected her. To get back at him, she made her husband send Joseph to prison.

During his time in prison, Joseph interpreted the dreams of two other prisoners. He was very good at it. One night, Pharaoh had a very strange dream. He dreamed that on the side of the Nile River, seven very fat cows were eating grass, when suddenly seven very thin cows came up out of the river and ate the fat cows.

Pharaoh was very upset by his dream and looked for someone who could explain his dream to him, but no one was able to do so. When Pharaoh found out that someone in prison could help him, he told the guards to fetch Joseph.

After Pharaoh had told Joseph about his dream, Joseph said, "Your dream means that for seven years Egypt will have lots and lots of food, but after that, for seven more years, the country will have no food. There is a lot of grain right now. It would be wise to store it for the difficult times." Pharaoh was so impressed by these words that he took Joseph out of prison and made him a governor.

The time came when there was not enough food, but in Egypt no one died from hunger thanks to the stored food. The food shortage affected the area where Joseph's father and brothers lived. Jacob told his sons, "Go to Egypt to buy some grain." All the brothers went except one, Benjamin, who stayed home to take care of his father.

In Egypt, the brothers went to the governor to buy grain. Joseph recognized his brothers straight away, but they did not recognize him. Because Joseph was still angry about what they had done to him, he put them in prison for three days. He then told them, "Go back home and get your youngest brother and bring him here. You may take food with you, but one of you must stay behind, to be sure you return." They did what had been asked, still not knowing Joseph's true identity.

Once they arrived with Benjamin, Joseph gave them the sacks of grain, but he hid a silver cup in one sack, so that they would be accused of stealing. When the guards discovered the cup, Joseph told the other brothers, "Benjamin has stolen it and as punishment, he must stay in prison in Egypt." The brothers were worried, and begged Joseph, "Take any one of us. Our father is already very old and has already lost one son. If he does not see Benjamin return, he will die!"

Seeing that his brothers were really upset, Joseph realized that they had changed and he revealed his true identity. "You did not recognize me, but I am your brother Joseph. I forgive you. Go and get our father and bring him here to Egypt so that we can all live happily together."

The brothers were very sorry for what they had done. They hugged each other and cried.

The Baby in the Basket

Joseph lived in peace with his brothers and his father in Egypt. The years went by, and they increased in number and became very powerful. They were known as Israelites, or Hebrews.

The new Pharaoh, however, was afraid that the Hebrews would take over his country. He made a law that forced Hebrews to be slaves. But even with these laws, the nation of Israel grew and grew.

So Pharaoh gave the order to kill all the Hebrew baby boys. One day, an Israelite woman gave birth to a strong and healthy boy. Because she was afraid that Pharaoh's men would kill him, she hid the baby for three months.

The mother feared that the crying of the baby would tell everyone where they were. She put the baby in a waterproof basket on the Nile River, hoping that someone would find her son and save him.

Miriam, the baby's sister, hid in the reeds to see where the basket would go. Pharaoh's daughter was swimming with her servant girls close by. Suddenly, she saw the basket and the baby. She said, "Maybe it is a Hebrew child. I will keep him with me, so the guards will not kill him."

Miriam decided to come out of her hiding place and talk with the princess, "Kind Princess, if you wish I can find a mother to raise the child." The princess answered, "Most certainly. I want to meet her." Miriam ran back home and told her mother what had happened.

The mother went straight to the princess who told her, "Raise this child for me, and I will pay you." The mother, full of joy, brought the baby back home. Once the child was old enough, he was brought back to the princess who took him in her arms and said, "I will call you Moses because I pulled you out of the water!"

The Ten Terrible Plagues

Moses was a happy child in Pharaoh's court, but he never forgot his family.

One day, Moses saw a very sad thing. An Egyptian was beating one of his people. Moses looked around to see if anyone was watching, then he killed the Egyptian and hid his body.

Moses realized what he had done and that Pharaoh would sentence him to death when he heard about it. Moses ran away and stayed in the desert for a very long time. He became a shepherd.

One day, while Moses was taking care of his sheep, he saw a bush that was on fire. The strange thing was that the bush didn't burn up. God spoke to Moses from the bush, "Go back to Egypt and free the Israelites. I will protect you. Take your people with you to a new land where you will all be free."

Moses and his brother, Aaron, went to Pharaoh and said, "God is ordering that you free the Israelites." Pharaoh replied, "No, get back to work. I do not know who God is." Pharaoh made the Israelites work even harder and did not free them.

Moses then said to Pharaoh, "I'm asking you, free the Hebrew nation, otherwise terrible plagues will fall upon Egypt." Once again, Pharaoh refused.

Just like Moses said, the plagues started to hit Egypt. First the water of the Nile changed into blood. The fish died and no one could drink water from the river. Then frogs came out of the river and invaded the whole of Egypt. They were everywhere; in the houses, the palace, everywhere. But Pharaoh still refused to listen to Moses.

After that, the dust of Egypt turned into gnats and swarmed on people and animals. But Pharaoh still refused to free the Israelites. Then the flies came. Swarms of flies invaded the whole land. Then God sent diseases that killed the Egyptian people's animals.

Once again, Pharaoh refused to free the Israelites.

The next plague covered the Egyptian people with sores. Then hail hit the ground hard and killed whoever was outside. Pharaoh, however, was very stubborn. He didn't let the Israelites go.

Locusts followed, eating all that was left on the trees and in the fields.

After that, the sun stopped shining and there was darkness for three days.

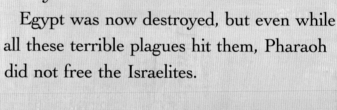

Egypt was now destroyed, but even while all these terrible plagues hit them, Pharaoh did not free the Israelites.

The worst plague was still to come. God warned Moses, "Tell every family of Israel to sacrifice a lamb and to mark the doors of their houses with the lamb's blood. Afterwards, the lamb needs to be roasted and eaten with bread made without yeast." The Hebrew people still remember this night and call it "Passover".

In the middle of the night, the eldest son of each Egyptian family died. The children of the Israelite families were spared.

The Israelites Leave Egypt

After the last plague had struck Egypt, Pharaoh freed the Israelites and they left Egypt.

Moses knew where to go, because God had sent a cloud to show them the way during the day, and fire to light their path at night.

Shortly after they had left, the Egyptian army chased the Israelites. Pharaoh wanted them back as slaves.

The Israelites had no place to hide and no way to escape. The army was about to catch up with them and in front of them lay the Red Sea.

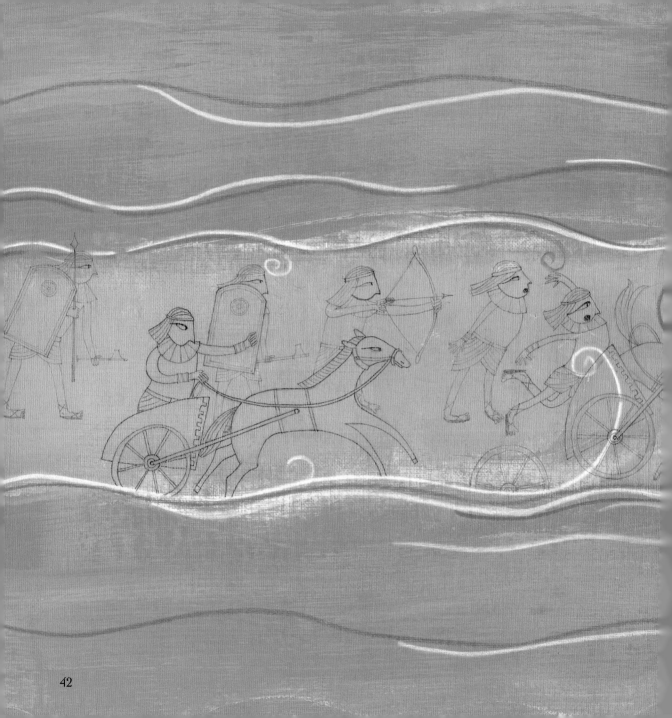

God told Moses, "Do not be afraid, tell the people to walk with you. Stretch out your hand over the sea." In the blink of an eye, the waters opened up, leaving a path for the Israelites to walk through. The Egyptian army was close behind.

When the entire nation of Israel had gone through, the sea closed and the Egyptians drowned. The people of Israel were free and safe at last.

The Ten Commandments

After walking across the desert, the Israelites arrived at Mount Sinai. Moses climbed the mountain to speak to God. God said, "I have led you here. Tell the people that if they obey Me, they will be My special people."

On the morning of the third day, they heard thunder and lightning. The sky suddenly became black and a trumpet blew in the distance. The Israelites trembled. They knew that God was coming.

The Lord called Moses to the top of the mountain to give him two stone tablets with the Ten Commandments written on them. Those were the rules the Israelites had to obey.

1. I am the Lord your God. Do not worship any other gods but Me.
2. Do not make any idols.
3. Keep the Lord's name holy.
4. Keep the Sabbath day holy.
5. Respect your father and mother.
6. Do not murder.
7. Keep marriage holy.
8. Do not steal.
9. Do not lie.
10. Do not desire anything belonging to your neighbor.

The Walls of Jericho

When Moses died, God chose Joshua to lead the
Israelites. He had to continue the journey to the
Promised Land.

   After crossing the Jordan River, the people of Israel
arrived at Jericho. But all around the city there were
very high walls.

   Joshua then spoke to God, "What must we do?"
The Lord answered, "March around the city once
a day for six days. The priests must carry trumpets
and walk in front of the Ark of the Covenant. On the
seventh day march around the city seven times and
tell the priests to blow their trumpets. The people
must also shout loudly when they hear the trumpets."

Joshua called the priests and army
together and told them what to do.
They did what God ordered.

On the seventh day the priests blew
the trumpets and the people shouted.
The walls of Jericho fell down and the
Israelites took over the city. Joshua
said, "God has given us power over
this city!"

Samson and Delilah

It did not take long for the Israelites to forget the rules of the Lord. The Philistines, an enemy nation, made slaves of them.

God, who is kind and loving, once again wanted to help His people.

One day, an angel appeared to an Israelite woman and told her that she was going to have a son. "You will have a strong son and he will free the Israelites from the Philistines, but remember to never cut his hair, because it is a sign that he belongs to God."

The woman and her husband called the baby Samson.

Samson was so strong that he killed a lion with his bare hands.

One day, Samson met a very beautiful Philistine girl, Delilah. He fell in love with her.

When the Philistine chiefs heard about this, they went behind Samson's back and asked the young woman to find out where Samson's strength came from. They promised to give her lots of money.

Every day, Delilah asked Samson for his secret, "If you love me, you will tell me."

So Samson eventually told her his secret, "My strength comes from my hair."

During the night, Delilah cut Samson's hair while he was sleeping. That is how Samson lost his strength.

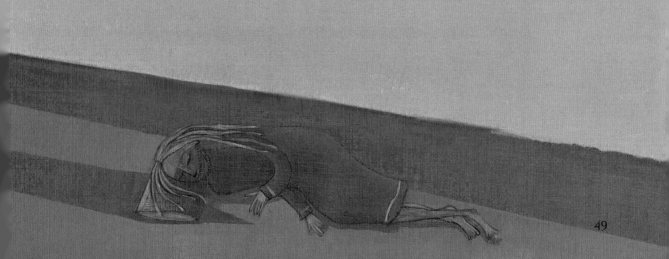

When the Philistine soldiers arrived at Samson's house, they poked his eyes out, making him blind, and threw him in prison. Samson was in prison for a long time. His hair grew, and he became strong again.

During a party, the Philistines, not knowing that Samson had become strong again, tied him to two pillars to make fun of him. As the Philistines laughed and made jokes about him, Samson put his left arm on one pillar and his right arm on the other one and said, "I will die with the Philistines!"

And that is exactly what happened. Samson pushed as hard as he could, causing the temple to collapse. The Philistines and Samson were buried under the weight of the walls. But Samson did not die for nothing. Through his death he brought back peace to the nation of Israel.

Ruth and Boaz

Ruth was a woman from the land of Moab. She belonged to an enemy nation of the Israelites, but she was good and kind.

Ruth was married to an Israelite and lived with her husband in Moab. She lived happily with him, his brother and his wife, Orpah, and her father-in-law and mother-in-law, Naomi. Then Ruth's husband, his brother and his father died.

Ruth and Orpah stayed with Naomi, who was now an old lady. Naomi decided to return to Bethlehem, her home land.

Naomi called Ruth and Orpah to tell them the news.

"My dear daughters-in-law, I am old. I want to go back to my country. There will be people to help me. You are young, don't worry about me. Go back to your families."

Orpah, in tears, did what her mother-in-law told her. Ruth, however, took Naomi's hand and said, "I do not want to leave you, I will go where you go. Your country will be my country. Your God will be my God."

Ruth and Naomi both went to Bethlehem at the beginning of the barley harvest. Before long, Ruth started working in a field. The fields she worked in belonged to Boaz, a very rich and powerful man.

One day, Boaz saw Ruth and asked the other workers, "Who is this woman?" They answered, "It is Ruth, Naomi's daughter-in-law."

So Boaz met Ruth and said, "Continue to harvest in these fields as much as you want. If you are thirsty, you can drink from the jugs of water." Ruth was surprised by his kindness and answered, "Why, my lord, are you so kind to me?" Boaz said, "Because you took care of Naomi and did not abandon her."

As time passed, Boaz realized that he was in love with Ruth.

As a relative of Naomi, Boaz was allowed to marry Ruth, but he wasn't the only one who could ask her to marry him. There was another relative who had more right to marry her. So Boaz talked to this relative.

Boaz asked, "Do you want to marry Ruth?"

And he replied, "I don't want to marry Ruth. I already have a family. I give you that right." And that is how Ruth and Boaz got married and lived happily together.

David Kills the Giant Goliath

David was the youngest son of Jesse. Every day, he took his father's sheep to graze. He spent most of his time playing music. He was kind but also very courageous. He had a sling which he used to protect the sheep from wolves and bears.

Three of David's older brothers were called by King Saul to go to war against the Philistines. David's father asked him to take food to his brothers, who were camping close by.

When David arrived the Philistines were about to attack. The Philistines had a champion fighter named Goliath. He was a giant. Everyone was very scared of him.

One of the Israelite soldiers told David, "This man comes to fight against Israel. The one who will kill him will be thanked by King Saul. He will also give him treasures and his daughter to marry." David said, "I will go and fight!" King Saul said, "But you are only a child!" "I am not afraid, God will protect me!" replied David.

Saul accepted, "Go and fight. I will give you my armor and my sword." But the king's armor was too heavy for David. He rather took his sling, picked up five round stones from the river and walked toward the Philistine. When Goliath saw David, he made fun of him, "You are crazy to come and fight with a sling. I will kill you." David answered, "You come to me with a sword, a spear and shield but I come to you in the name of the Lord!" David released a stone and hit the giant on his forehead.

Goliath fell to the ground. David then jumped on the giant and killed him with Goliath's own sword. The Philistines ran away. The Israelites won!

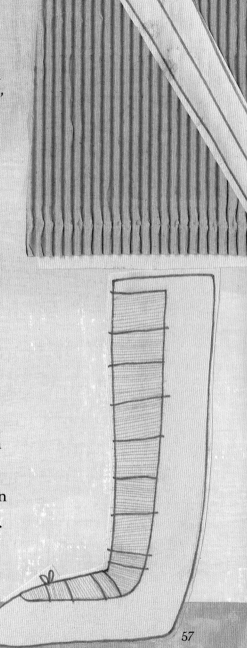

57

Wise King Solomon

When Solomon became king of Israel, the kingdom became very rich and powerful. The people loved Solomon for his great wisdom.

One day, two women came to him for help to solve an argument. One of them said, "We live in the same house, and we both gave birth a few days ago. But this woman's son died. After that, she came to my room and took my baby from his cradle, and put her dead baby in his place."

And the other woman answered, "This is not true, my son is alive and your son is dead."

King Solomon then ordered a soldier, "Take a sword, cut the child in two and give half to each woman." Before the soldier could take out his sword, the child's real mother, with tears in her eyes, cried out, "Please Master, I beg you. Do not kill the child." And pointing to the other woman, she continued, "Rather give the baby to her!"

The king then knew who the real mother was and said, "Give the child to that woman, she is the mother. Only the real mother will protect her son like that."

The Queen of Sheba Visits King Solomon

The powerful Queen of Sheba heard about Solomon's wisdom, and came to test him with difficult questions. She arrived in Jerusalem, where Solomon lived, with a lot of camels loaded with gold and precious stones. As soon as she met Solomon, she asked him very difficult questions, but he answered all of them.

The Queen of Sheba was impressed by Solomon's wisdom. But she was also impressed with his kingdom and his wealth. "I have heard of your great wisdom, but I did not believe it. That is the reason I came to see you with my own eyes. But what is said about you does not even match half of your greatness."

"Your nation should be glad because they can hear your words. And blessed be the Lord your God, who gave you all these gifts and who made you king of Israel."

Then the queen left. She gave Solomon amazing gifts of gold, precious stones and spices, as well as precious wood. With the wood, Solomon made instruments for his singers, and built strong balconies in the temple to the glory of God.

Three Brave Men in the Fiery Furnace

The king of Babylon, Nebuchadnezzar, asked for a huge statue of gold to be built. When it was completed, he wanted to show it to everyone, inviting all the leaders from all his kingdom's provinces. They were all looking at the statue when one of the high commanders said, "This law is for all of you. When you hear the sound of musical instruments, everyone must bow in front of the statue that Nebuchadnezzar has built. Whoever does not obey will be thrown into the fiery furnace."

The people were scared and did what had been ordered. Every time they heard the music, they bowed before the statue.

One day, someone reported to the king that three Jews, Shadrach, Meshach and Abednego, living in the province of Babylon, hadn't obeyed and worshiped the statue. The king called them and said, "Is it true that you do not worship my statue? If this is so, you will be thrown into a blazing furnace."

The young men answered, "We don't need to defend ourselves. The God we serve will save us from the fiery furnace."

Nebuchadnezzar became angry and ordered that the furnace be heated seven times hotter than usual.

Then he ordered his strongest soldiers to chain the three young men up and throw them into the furnace.

The soldiers did what the king had ordered. But the three young men walked around in the middle of the fire without being burnt.

Daniel in the Lions' Den

After Nebuchadnezzar died, Belshazzar became king. He was a very cruel man. One evening, the king had a great feast in his palace and ordered his slaves to bring gold and silver cups to drink wine. These cups were stolen by Nebuchadnezzar from the temple in Jerusalem.

As the king and his guests were drinking from these cups, the fingers of a human hand wrote words on the wall that no one could understand. The king was very scared. He ordered for wizards and magicians across his kingdom to tell him what was written on the wall, but no one could read it.

They called in a Jew named Daniel, who was known to have great knowledge and understanding and who could interpret dreams and solve difficult problems.

The words written on the wall were:

MENE, MENE, TEKEL, UPHARSIN

"The first part means that God has put an end to your time as king, the second part says that He has weighed you on scales and has found you not good enough, and the third part says that your kingdom will be divided and given to the Medes and the Persians."

Belshazzar, impressed by this explanation, ordered that Daniel become the third highest ruler in the kingdom.

That same night, Belshazzar was killed and his kingdom was given to Darius the Mede. Daniel became one of the three supervisors of the kingdom. Because the king admired his wisdom, he considered making Daniel the leader of the whole kingdom.

The other leaders were jealous of Daniel's power. They also knew that he believed in God. They organized a plan to make him lose everything. They asked the king to make a new law. They said, "O Darius, you are our king and we are your faithful servants. You must make a law that will forbid anyone to pray, to humans or gods, except to you. Whoever disobeys you will be thrown into the lions' den."

When Daniel heard about the law, he didn't stop praying to God. Spies discovered that he was still praying and they told the king. Darius was upset and tried everything possible to save Daniel, but the law could not be changed. Daniel was thrown into the lions' den.

Darius was very sad and told Daniel, "My friend, I hope that your God will save you." During the night, the king was worried and could not sleep. He waited until the morning to know if Daniel had survived.

As the sun rose, Darius ran to the lions' den and saw that Daniel was alive. Daniel told the king, "O King, God sent an angel to close the lions' mouths because I was innocent in His eyes."

The king ordered that Daniel be taken out of the lions' den, and instead threw the people who had unfairly accused Daniel into the lions' den.

Jonah and the Big Fish

One day, God spoke to man a named Jonah and told him, "Go to the city of Nineveh and tell the people that they have sinned against Me."

But Jonah did not listen to the Lord and tried to run away. He hid on a ship sailing to Tarshish, in the opposite direction of Nineveh. God, who sees everything, made a big storm on the sea just after the ship left the harbor.

The sailors were terrified and prayed that the ship would not sink. The captain of the ship found Jonah sleeping and woke him up. He told him, "Instead of sleeping, call upon your God to protect us and not let us die."

Jonah knew that it was his fault, so he told the sailors, "God is angry with me. That is why we are in trouble. Throw me into the sea so the storm can stop."

The sailors threw Jonah overboard. The storm stopped immediately. God sent a big fish to swallow Jonah.

Jonah stayed three days and three nights in the fish's stomach where he prayed to God, "In great danger I have called upon the Lord, and He has listened to me. He saved me from the waters of the sea when I thought that I was going to die!"

God ordered the whale to spit Jonah out on the beach. Then God told Jonah, "This time, go to Nineveh and do what I have asked."

Jonah obeyed. He went to Nineveh and told the people, "If you do not repent, God will destroy your city." The king of Nineveh, terrified by those words, ordered a fast. "Everyone, even the animals, must stop eating. We have sinned, but maybe God will have mercy on us and forgive us." God saw that the people was sorry and He forgave them.

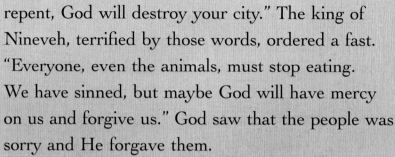

But Jonah was mad that God changed his mind. "You are too good, merciful and forgiving. Now, I am asking you to kill me, because I would prefer to be dead." God answered, "You don't have the right to be angry."

70

So Jonah left the town and stayed on a nearby hill to see what would happen to the city.

God made a vine grow quickly so that Jonah could have some shade. This made Jonah very happy. But the next day God sent a worm to eat the vine, and He made the weather very hot.

Jonah no longer had any shade and became very weak. He wanted to die. The Lord said, "You are crying about a vine that you did not plant or take care of. Should I not have mercy on the people that I made?"

The New Testament

An Angel Visits Mary

In Nazareth, in the land of Galilee, lived a young woman named Mary. She was engaged to Joseph.

One day, an angel sent by God appeared to Mary. The angel Gabriel came to tell her great news, "Greetings, Mary, the Lord is with you!"

Mary was confused but the angel told her, "Do not be afraid, Mary. I have come to tell you that you will give birth to a son, and you must name Him Jesus. He will be called the Son of God, and He will come to earth to save people from all evil, and He will rule forever."

Mary answered, "How can I have a son if I am not married?" The angel explained, "The Holy Spirit will come upon you."

Mary then said, "I am here. I am the servant of the Lord, may what you have said to me come true."

When Joseph found out that Mary was pregnant, he wondered if he should still marry her. While Joseph was thinking about this, an angel spoke to him in his dreams, and told him, "Joseph, do not be afraid. The baby that Mary will have is from the Holy Spirit. Name the baby Jesus, because He will save the people from their sins." So Joseph knew that God had spoken to him. Not long after that he married Mary.

Baby Jesus Is Born

Joseph and Mary were joyfully waiting for the birth of Jesus. When Mary was about to give birth, the Roman emperor Augustus made a law. All the people had to go back to the town where they were born to be counted.

Joseph came from Bethlehem, so he had to travel there with Mary to be counted.

When they arrived in Bethlehem, Mary knew that it was time to give birth. Joseph knocked on the door of a hotel, but the owner said there were no rooms available.

Mary and Joseph had to sleep in a stable with animals. Mary gave birth to a son. She wrapped Him in a blanket and laid Him in a manger.

Not very far from the village, shepherds were looking after their flocks. Suddenly, an angel of the Lord appeared to them and said, "Today your Savior has been born. You will find a child in a stable. Go and praise Him."

Then the shepherds went to Bethlehem and found the child the angel told them about. After they saw Baby Jesus, they returned to their country to tell everyone about His birth.

79

The Wise Men Visit Baby Jesus

Wise men from the East arrived in Jerusalem to praise the Son of God. They asked around, "Where is the baby who has been born to be the King of the Jews? We are looking for Him so we can worship Him. When He was born, a new star appeared in the sky, much brighter than all the others, and it guided us from very far to this place."

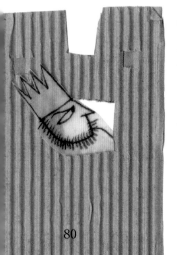

King Herod was worried when he heard the news, as were all the people in Jerusalem. Herod told the wise men, "Go and find out where Jesus is. When you find Him, let me know, so that I can also worship Him."

The truth was that Herod was afraid of Jesus, and wanted to kill Him. When the wise men arrived in Bethlehem, the star stopped at the place where Jesus was sleeping.

They kneeled down and gave Him gifts of gold, frankincense and myrrh.

That night, an angel appeared to the wise men in a dream and said, "Do not go back to Herod, because he wants to kill Jesus."

Early the next morning, the wise men left the kingdom to return to their country. They didn't tell Herod where Jesus was. That same night, an angel appeared in a dream to Joseph and told him, "Quick, wake up, take your son and Mary and go to Egypt. You will stay there until I say it is safe, because Herod wants to kill Jesus and is looking for Him."

Joseph left straight away with his wife and child. At the same time, Herod, who realized that the wise men had left without telling him, sent his soldiers to Bethlehem and ordered them to kill all the baby boys under the age of two. But Jesus was safely on His way to Egypt.

Once Herod died, an angel appeared to Joseph to let him know that it was safe to go back to Israel. Joseph returned with Mary and Jesus and lived in the town of Nazareth. That is why Jesus was called "The Nazarene".

Joseph and Mary Find Jesus in the Temple

Jesus was growing up peacefully, protected by the deep love of Joseph and Mary. Jesus went to school in Nazareth and became very smart as He grew older.

When He turned twelve, He went to Jerusalem with His parents for Passover.

After the celebration, His parents left.

They were already on their way back home when they realized that Jesus was not with them. They were very worried and returned to Jerusalem to look for Him.

After three days, they found Him sitting in the temple, discussing the Scriptures with the teachers. Surprised, Joseph and Mary ran to Him and said, "We were so worried about You! Why have You done this?"

And Jesus replied, "I did not want you to worry, but why were you looking for Me? Do you not know that I must take care of the work of My Father?"

Jesus returned to Nazareth with His parents where He spent His childhood loving and respecting God and His family.

Jesus Is Baptized

When Jesus was an adult, He went to the Jordan River to see John the Baptist. John preached the word of God and baptized people.

At the river, Jesus asked John to baptize Him. But John replied, "You come to me, but it is me who should be baptized by You."

Jesus answered, "I'm asking you, John. We should do all the things that are God's will."

And John did as he was asked.

When Jesus was baptized, heaven opened, and Jesus saw the Spirit of God coming down on Him like a dove. Then the voice of God could be heard in the skies, "You are My dear Son, and I am pleased with You."

The Twelve Disciples

Jesus traveled across Galilee preaching the word of God and healing the sick.

Everywhere He went crowds followed Him and came to listen to what He had to say.

The news about Jesus' miracles spread far and wide, and many people came to see Jesus. He healed them and cared for them.

    One day, while
Jesus was walking along
the beach by the Sea of Galilee,
He saw two fishermen, Simon Peter and
his brother Andrew, who were throwing
their nets into the water. They were
fishermen. Jesus said to them, "Come with
Me, and I will show you how to fish for people."
    They left their nets and followed Him.
    As Jesus was walking a bit farther, He saw two other fishermen,
two brothers as well, James and John, and their father, Zebedee. He called
these two brothers. Immediately they left their boat and followed Jesus.

Jesus then called more men to follow Him. Jesus chose twelve disciples. Their names were Simon, whom Jesus later called Peter, Andrew, James and John sons of Zebedee, Philip, Bartholomew, Thomas, Matthew, James son of Alphaeus, Thaddaeus, Simon, and Judas Iscariot.

Jesus called them so that He could send them to preach to the people.

Simon   James son   Bartholomew   Andrew   Peter
         of Alphaeus

Jesus told them, "Go and tell everyone that the kingdom of God is near. Help and heal the poor and the sick, without asking for anything in return. Do not seek money. Your mission will not be easy because there are a lot of bad people who will not believe your words. They will hate you because of Me. But do not be afraid, because it is the Spirit of God the Father who will speak for you."

Thomas   Matthew   Judas Iscariot   John   James son   Philip   Thaddaeus
                                                                        of Zebedee

The Wedding at Cana

Jesus and His disciples were invited to a wedding in the village of Cana, in Galilee.

Jesus' mother, Mary, was also at the wedding.

While everyone was enjoying the wedding feast, the wine ran out. So Mary told Jesus, who answered, "Mother, why are you worried? My time has not yet come." Mary told the servants, "Do whatever Jesus tells you to do."

A few water jars stood nearby. Jesus told the servants, "Fill these jars with water and take them to the bridegroom." When the master of the feast tasted it, it had changed into wine.

The guests enjoyed the good wine and were thankful to the host, "Usually people start with the best wine. But you have kept the best wine for last!"

Jesus Preaches to the People

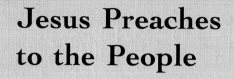

Jesus and His disciples spent their days helping the poor, telling them how good God is. Big crowds gathered around the Son of God to listen to Him.

One day, a crowd was waiting for Jesus to speak. He came down from the mountain, and when He sat down, He started talking to the people:

"Blessed are the poor, because the kingdom of God belongs to them.

Blessed are those who are hungry, because they will have plenty to eat.

Blessed are those who cry, because they will be comforted.

God will bless you when people hurt you and talk badly of you because of Me. Be happy because you will have many rewards in the kingdom of heaven.

You are the light of the world. Your light will shine so that others can see what you do and give thanks to God.

Love your enemies; bless those who curse you, and pray for those who hurt you.

If someone hits you on your right cheek, turn your left cheek also.

Forgive others like your Father forgives.

Do not judge and you will not be judged.

Do not be hard on others, and God won't be hard on you.

Forgive and you will be forgiven."

Then Jesus told them a story: "Whoever hears My words and do what I say will be like a wise man who builds his house on a rock. The rain will fall, the wind will blow, but his house will not fall because it has been built on a rock. On the other hand, whoever hears My words and does not do what I say is like a man who builds his house on the sand. The rain will fall, the wind will blow, and his house will be washed away."

Jesus Gives Food to a Big Crowd

A very big crowd came to listen to Jesus. It was already late when the disciples told Him, "There is no food here and it is late. Tell these people to go back to the villages to buy some food."

But Jesus asked, "Why don't you give them food to eat?"

They answered, "We have only five loaves of bread and two fish. It will not be enough!"

Jesus then told the crowd to sit down on the grass. He took the bread and the fish and, looking up to heaven, He thanked God for the food. Then Jesus broke the bread and gave it to the disciples who shared it among the crowd.

The bread and the fish kept on multiplying. Jesus had performed a miracle! The disciples could feed five thousand men, as well as the women and children. And they had twelve baskets of leftovers.

Jesus Walks on Water

After Jesus had performed the miracle of the bread and fish, He told His disciples to get into a boat that was close to them and go to the other side of the lake. He told the crowd to return home. Jesus then went up a mountain to pray by Himself.

That evening, Jesus walked on the water toward His disciples who were waiting in the boat.

When the disciples saw Him walking on the water, they were terrified and shouted, "It is a ghost!" Jesus told them, "Do not be afraid, it is Me." Peter wanted to go to Jesus, so Jesus said, "Come to Me."

Peter walked on the water, but the wind started to blow. Peter got scared and started to sink. He shouted, "Lord, save me!"

Jesus gave Peter His hand and said, "You don't have much faith. Why do you doubt?" When they climbed back into the boat, the other disciples went down on their knees in front of Jesus and said, "You are really the Son of God!"

Jesus Teaches What Is Important

Jesus was in Jerusalem, and very clever teachers of the Law were talking to Him about God, trying to test Him. One of them asked, "What is the most important commandment?"

Jesus answered, "Love the Lord your God with all your heart, soul, mind and strength. It is the first and the most important of all the commandments. And the second one is close to the first, 'Love your neighbors as much as you love yourself.' There are no greater commandments than these."

The Good Samaritan

One day, a teacher of the law tested Jesus' wisdom and asked Him, "Master, what must I do to have eternal life?" Jesus replied, "What is written in the Scriptures?"

The teacher of the law answered, "Love the Lord your God, with all your heart, soul, and strength, and love your neighbors as much as you love yourself."

Jesus said, "You have given the right answer. Do that and you will live." The teacher of the law then asked Him, "Who is my neighbor?"

Jesus told him a story, "A man was traveling to Jericho. On his journey, a group of thieves attacked him and stole all his belongings." A priest walked on that same path and pretended not to see the man, leaving him lying on the ground.

Soon afterwards another man who worked in the temple of Jerusalem walked by without looking at him. But a Samaritan saw the man and stopped to help him. He bandaged his wounds and put him on his donkey. Then the Samaritan took the man to a hotel and took care of him.

The next day, he paid the hotelkeeper to take care of the man, and left.

In your opinion, which one of these three people has loved their neighbor like himself?"

And the teacher of the law replied, "The Samaritan."

Jesus told him, "Now go and do what he did."

Jesus Brings Lazarus Back to Life

Lazarus lived in Bethany. He was a friend of Jesus, and he was very sick.

Martha and Mary, Lazarus's sisters, sent a message asking Jesus to come and heal him. But Jesus did not go straight away. He answered, "By his sickness, the Son of God will be glorified."

A few days later, Jesus told His disciples, "Our friend Lazarus is sleeping, but I am going to wake him up!"

The disciples answered, "If he is sleeping, he will get better." Jesus really meant that Lazarus was dead. Jesus then told them plainly, "Lazarus is not sleeping. He is dead. And now you will see how amazing God is."

Jesus went to Bethany with His disciples. Lazarus had been buried in a tomb for four days. When Martha saw Jesus, she told Him, "Lord, if You had come earlier, my brother would not be dead!"

Jesus answered her, "Your brother will live again. I am the one who raises the dead to life. Whoever believes in Me will not die. Do you believe that?"

And Martha said, "Yes, You are the Son of God."

Then Jesus saw that Mary was crying because her brother had died. He said, "Take Me to the place where your brother is buried."

When Jesus arrived at the tomb, He told the people to move the big stone away from the entrance.

After the stone had been rolled away, Jesus looked up to heaven and said, "Father, thank You for answering my prayers."

Then He shouted, "Lazarus, come out!"

Lazarus came out of the tomb alive. Jesus had performed another miracle.

The Lord's Prayer

One day, Jesus was praying when one of His disciples asked Him, "Lord, will You teach us how to pray the way You do?"

And Jesus replied, "When you pray say these words:

'Our Father in heaven,

May Your name always be kept holy,

May Your kingdom come,

and what You want be done,

on earth as in heaven.

Give us the food we need for each day.

Forgive us our sins

Just as we have forgiven those who sinned against us.

And do not allow us to be tempted,

But save us from the Evil One.

Amen.'"

Then He added, "Ask, and you will receive, search and you will find, knock and the door will be opened for you. Which father would give a stone to his son if he asks for bread? Even if you are bad, you know how to give good things to your children. How much more then will the Father in heaven not give good gifts to those who ask Him."

The Prodigal Son

One day, Jesus told a story, "A rich man had two sons. The youngest son told his father, 'Father, give me my share of the inheritance.' And his father gave it to him.

The youngest son took his money and left for a country far away. There he wasted all his money. When every penny had been spent and he had nothing to eat, a great famine came over the land. He found a job feeding pigs on a farm. He was starving, but the pigs had enough to eat. He ate the leftovers and thought to himself, *My father's workers have plenty to eat, and here I am starving to death. I will go back to my father, I will ask for his forgiveness and I will beg him to take me in and treat me like one of his workers.*

So the son left and went back to his father. His father saw him and was very glad. He ran to him and hugged him.

The son told his father, 'Father, I am no longer good enough to be called your son because I have behaved badly.'

But the father told his servants, 'Bring the best clothes and put them on him. Then get ready for a great feast to celebrate my son's return.'

The eldest son became angry with his father and said, 'For all these years, I have always behaved well and obeyed you. You have never had a feast for me. But when my brother, who has wasted all your money, comes back, you welcome him with a great feast.'

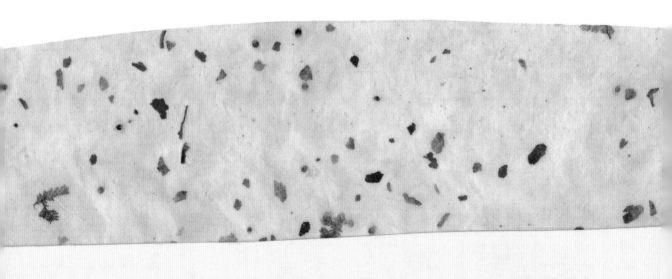

The father answered, 'My son, you are always with me, and what belongs to me belongs to you. But we should be glad and celebrate because your brother has come home safely.'"

Jesus and the Children

Some people brought their children to Jesus so that He could bless them and pray for them. But the disciples told them to go away, "Leave Jesus in peace!"

But Jesus said, "Let the little children come to Me, because the kingdom of God is for those who are like them."

Jesus Goes to Jerusalem

When Jesus and His disciples reached Jerusalem, near the Mount of Olives, Jesus told one of His disciples, "Go to the next village and bring Me a donkey."

The disciple left and found the donkey. They led the donkey to Jesus. They put a cloak on its back, and Jesus rode the donkey. That was how Jesus arrived in Jerusalem. The people who were following the Son of God spread their coats out on the road, while others cut branches from the trees.

Everyone was singing, "Blessed is the One who comes in the name of the Lord."

When Jesus had passed through the gates of Jerusalem, the people living in the town were surprised and asked, "Who is this person?"

And the crowd answered,

"It is Jesus, the prophet from Nazareth in Galilee."

117

Jesus' Last Supper

It was almost Passover, and the disciples asked Jesus, "Master, where do You want us to prepare the Passover meal?"

Jesus answered, "Go into Jerusalem, and follow a man carrying a water jug. He will show you a big room. That is the place where we will celebrate Passover."

The disciples did what Jesus asked. That evening, Jesus sat with them at the table. As they were eating, Jesus said, "One of you will certainly turn against Me." The disciples were very sad, and each one asked Jesus, "Lord, will it be me?"

Even Judas asked, "Will it be me?" Jesus answered, "Yes, it is you."

Judas knew that Jesus was right. Just before the supper Judas had gone to see the priests who wanted to kill Jesus. They were concerned about Jesus' growing power over the people. They made a deal with Judas to turn Jesus in for a sum of money. He would show them who Jesus was by kissing Him on the cheek.

While they were still eating, Jesus said, "I am happy to be with you tonight, because it is the last time we will be together."

Then Jesus took the bread and broke it and gave it to the disciples saying, "Take this and eat it, it is My body."

Then He took a cup of wine, lifted it up to heaven and gave it to the disciples, "All of you drink this, because it is My blood, poured out to save people from their sins."

When the dinner was finished, Judas left. The other disciples sang songs to the glory of God, and then walked to the Mount of Olives. Jesus told Peter, "This night, you will all abandon Me." And Peter answered, "Lord, I will never abandon you!"

Jesus replied, "My dear Peter, before the rooster crows twice you will say three times that you don't know Me."

Peter was confused by these words.

121

Jesus Prays in the Garden of Gethsemane

Jesus went with His disciples to the Garden of Gethsemane and told them to sit down and wait for Him while He prayed.

He took Peter, James and John with Him and said, "I am very sad. Stay awake with Me."

He walked away to one side and prayed, "My Father, may Your will be done!"

When Jesus came back, He found His three disciples asleep. He asked, "Couldn't you stay awake with Me for one hour? Pray that you won't be tested." Then He returned to pray some more.

Later He went back to the three disciples and saw that they were sleeping again and He said, "Are you still sleeping? My time is up. The Son of God is going to be handed over to sinners. Here comes the one who will betray Me."

Jesus Is Arrested

Jesus was still speaking when Judas appeared, followed by a large number of soldiers with swords and clubs. Judas walked up to Jesus, kissed Him and told the soldiers, "This is Jesus."

The soldiers grabbed Jesus and arrested Him. Then Peter took out his sword and cut off a soldier's ear, but Jesus healed the soldier immediately, saying, "Enough! Put your sword away."

Jesus said to all those who wanted to arrest Him, "You have come with weapons as if you're coming to arrest a thief. I have spoken so many times in the temple and you have never tried to arrest Me. But this is the way it must happen."

Jesus was captured and the disciples ran away, just like He had predicted.

Peter Says He Doesn't Know Jesus

Jesus was taken to Caiaphas, the high priest, to be questioned. Peter secretly followed Jesus and hid outside.

A servant girl saw Peter, "You were with Jesus," she said. Peter denied it and answered, "No, not at all!"

Another servant girl pointed at Peter, "He was with Jesus of Nazareth." Peter denied it again, "I do not know that man!"

A little while later, a group of people said, "He is one of Jesus' disciples." So Peter started to shout, "I do not know who Jesus is!"

At that moment, the rooster crowed, and Peter remembered Jesus' words. He started to cry because he knew that he had turned his back on his Master.

Jesus and Pilate

The priests and religious leaders decided that Jesus should die. They took Him to the Roman governor Pontius Pilate. He asked Jesus if it was true what people said, that He was the King of the Jews.

Jesus answered, "Those are your own words."

The priests accused Jesus of being a liar. Pilate asked, "Don't You hear what crimes they say You have done?"

But Jesus did not say anything.

Pilate did not really know what to do with Jesus, because he knew that Jesus was innocent. He had been arrested by jealous priests.

During Passover the governor always freed one prisoner chosen by the people.

Pilate asked the crowd, "Which prisoner do you want me to set free? Barabbas, a murder, or Jesus, who is called the Messiah?"

And the people shouted, "Barabbas!"

Pilate added, "And what must I do with Jesus?"

The people answered, "Crucify Him!"

Pilate said, "But what has He done to deserve it?"

And the people replied louder, "Nail Him to a cross!"

So Pilate ordered his soldiers to beat Jesus with a whip and nail Him to a cross.

Jesus Carries His Cross to Golgotha

The soldiers took Jesus to the yard in the middle of the palace and put a red robe on Him. They made a crown of thorns for His head, and put a staff in His hand. Then they hit Him and made fun of Him. "Here is the one who thinks He is the King of the Jews!" they said.

They put Jesus' clothes back on and made Him carry a huge cross made of wood all the way to Golgotha.

Jesus was tired and covered with blood. He fell many times, but the soldiers forced Him to get up by hitting Him.

A great crowd gathered around Him and cried for Jesus, because He was suffering.

Jesus Dies and Is Buried

When Jesus arrived at Golgotha, the soldiers nailed His hands and feet to a wooden cross. To make fun of Him, they wrote on the top of the cross: "This is Jesus, the King of the Jews."

Two robbers were crucified beside Jesus, one on the left, and one on the right. One of them said mean things to Jesus. The other one talked to Him, begging for mercy, "Lord, please remember me when You are in Your kingdom."

And Jesus answered, "Do not worry. Today you will be with Me in Paradise."

A crowd gathered around Jesus. At His feet was His mother, Mary, and His disciple John. Mary could not stop crying. Jesus told John, "My dear John, take care of My mother." And, from that day, Mary lived in John's home.

Then Jesus said, "I am thirsty." One of the soldiers put a sponge dipped in wine to Jesus' mouth but He did not drink. Around midday, the sky turned black and the ground started to shake. This meant that Jesus was dead.

The crowd became afraid and ran away. One of the soldiers said, "Look at the sky. Surely this man was really God's Son!"

It was Friday evening and Jesus' body was taken off the cross, wrapped in a sheet and put in a tomb carved in a mountain. The entrance to the tomb was closed with a big rock.

Mary Magdalene Sees Jesus Alive

On the Sunday morning, a friend of Jesus, Mary Magdalene, and two other women went to Jesus' tomb, but when they arrived, they noticed that the big rock had been rolled away.

They went inside the tomb and saw that it was empty. Afraid, they went quickly to Peter and John, who ran to see the empty tomb with their own eyes. They couldn't believe it. They wondered what had happened to Jesus.

Mary Magdalene stayed close to the tomb and cried. Then she saw a man walking toward her. It was Jesus, but she did not recognize Him at first. Jesus asked Mary, "Why are you crying?"

Mary replied, "Because they have taken away my Lord!"

Jesus said to her, "Mary, do you not recognize Me?"

Suddenly she understood everything and said, "My Master!" Then, with her heart full of joy, she went to tell the disciples that she had seen Jesus.

The Road to Emmaus

That same evening, two friends of Jesus left Jerusalem to go to the village of Emmaus. As they were walking, they talked about what had happened to Jesus.

Along the way, Jesus joined them and asked, "What are you talking about?"

The two friends, who did not recognize Him, answered in a sad voice, "Jesus of Nazareth was tortured and killed by the Romans." And they told Him everything that had happened.

When they arrived at Emmaus, the two friends invited Jesus to eat with them. As they sat at the table, they finally realized that the man was Jesus, but He disappeared.

The two friends hurried to Jerusalem to tell the disciples what had happened. When they were all together, Jesus appeared to them and said, "Peace be with you!"

The men were very afraid because they thought they had seen a ghost. But Jesus told them, "Do not be afraid, it really is Me; touch Me and you will see."

Then Jesus asked to eat with them.

Before He left, Jesus told them, "I had to die so that I could come back to life on the third day. That was the will of God, My Father.

Whoever believes in Me and in God will be forgiven. Go and tell everyone around the world."

Jesus Goes Back to Heaven

After Jesus ate with the disciples, He blessed them. Then, with light shining all around Him, He was taken up into heaven.

The disciples, crying with joy, waved at Him. They returned to Jerusalem to tell everyone that Jesus had risen from the dead and that He was now with His Father in heaven.

ABOUT THE ILLUSTRATIONS
by Martino Signoretto, priest and biblical scholar

Dear parents, in this Bible for children, the words and the illustrations go hand in hand. Each illustration shows something of God's divine mystery. I would like to explain how the stories and the illustrations are linked together in the following explanations. Take note of the bold words.

THE OLD TESTAMENT

From the book of Genesis: the origins of life on earth and God's people

God Creates the World (1:1-25)

God created light. It represents a divine light that shines from the center of the world and radiates beauty. The light is like the **word of God**: it illuminates, it communicates, and it creates. This is why the words in the illustration on page 8-9 are at the center of the earth. They are also the first **words** in the Bible. The sun and moon are in the corners of the picture. They have been created after the **light**.

The world is imagined as a **garden** of harmony (p. 10-11). The wolf grazes in the field, the lamb is not afraid of the wolf, Eve strokes a crocodile. In short, there is no need to shed blood in order to find food. **Peace** reigns and everything is in harmony.

Adam and Eve (1:26-31; 2-3)

The **Garden** is a magnificent place, it is a gift from God. The man and woman are free, but they are at risk of spoiling it all. The **snake**, a cunning animal, has poisonous words that create doubt that God might be playing with **Adam and Eve**. He causes a rift between them and seduces them. They eat the forbidden fruit, spoiling the gift. The gates of the **Garden** are closed and **evil** starts to spread in the world.

Cain Kills His Brother Abel (4)

The two brothers are very different from each other. In the picture (p. 14-15), the yellow background surrounds Abel with **light**, while the dark background symbolizes Cain's jealousy. Envy enters Cain's heart and leads him to kill his own brother!

Noah Builds a Big Boat (5-8)

After man's first sin, **evil** started to spread. So God designed a big "safety boat" – **Noah's Ark**. In the illustration (p. 16-17), the boat is so big that it goes beyond the page, showing that there is enough space for Noah's family and all the animals. A **dove** marks the end of the flood, carrying in its beak an olive branch, a symbol of peace (p. 19).

The Tower of Babel (11)

The **tower** in the picture (p. 20-21), is so tall that you cannot see the beginning or the end, much like God.

How does God react? He does not send a flood, but He makes the people speak different languages. In this way, the people discovered that they cannot regroup in a single empire, talk the same language, dress the same way; that is why they are **dressed differently**. To live in peace, they must learn to understand each other.

Abraham and Sarah (12-13)

God can never be defeated, and He chooses a humble shepherd, Abraham, to bring into being His future people. God asks Abraham to be courageous. He must start out on a very long **journey**. Even if Abraham's wife, Sarah, could not have any children, God promises him many descendants, as numerous as the **stars** in the sky, as we can see in the illustration (p. 22-23).

After the birth of his son, Abraham is tested. God asks him to sacrifice the gift he has received, his son. But just before he does, God stops him. In the illustration, you can see a ram **hidden** behind the mountain which Abraham cannot see (p. 23). The ram will be sacrificed instead of Isaac.

God Finds a Wife for Isaac (21-24)

Isaac grew up and the time to get married arrived. A servant helped him to find a wife. The servant went on a **trip** and stopped next to a **well**, where women were chatting and collecting water. He met the beautiful **Rebekah**, who agreed to become Isaac's future wife.

Joseph the Dreamer (37-45)

Joseph was a great dreamer! He dreamt that eleven stars, the sun and the moon bowed down to him. The stars were his brothers. The **sun** and the **moon** were his parents. The dream is the premonition of what would happen when they would have to kneel in front of Joseph in Egypt, once he became governor.

From the book of Exodus: a nation saved from slavery

The Baby in the Basket (1-6)

Moses is saved from being killed. His mother hid him in a **basket** on the Nile River. A great destiny awaited him.

In Egypt, he will become a very powerful man. See the illustration on page 36-37: He is close to a sacred bush that "burns without consuming itself". Moses will become a man of God because he will meet the divine **light**.

The Ten Terrible Plagues (7-11)

Moses had an important mission: to save God's people from slavery in Egypt. In the illustration on page 38-39, Moses, is depicted as inferior to Pharaoh; smaller and at the bottom of the page. But the drawing of him is in a light color, depicting that he is in the **light**. He will have to face the powerful Pharaoh, who, just like **Cain**, is portrayed in dark colors. The **hieroglyphs**, under the throne of Pharaoh are significant as well: they represent the **ten plagues** that will hit Egypt because of Pharaoh's refusal to let the people go (p. 39).

The Israelites Leave Egypt (12-14)

Eventually, the Israelites were freed from slavery, but there was a problem. **Evil** followed them, represented by the **crowd of enemies**, the Egyptians, pursuing them (p. 42-43). But the Israelites did not drown because God made a way for them to escape.

The Ten Commandments (20)

Moses took his people to Mount Sinai, where the **earth and the sky almost met** as depicted in the illustration on page 44-45. Only Moses was allowed up the mountain because he was a man of God. The people stayed at the bottom and waited for Moses, who received the Ten Commandments from God. They are in actual fact precious words of freedom.

*From the book of **Joshua**: destroying the walls of a fortified city*

The Walls of Jericho (5-6)

How can you destroy the **huge walls** of a fortified city? With the sound of God's **trumpets** and with His **Word**, we can destroy any wall of fear.

*From the book of **Judges**: to lose the gift of strength because of naivety*

Samson and Delilah (13-16)

Samson was strong and courageous, but in the illustration on page 49, the **shadow of the sword** is already touching his hair, the source of his strength, hinting that he might indeed lose his strength. But he will regain it at the end of his life because he will call on the help of the Lord.

*From the book of **Ruth**: the courage of leaving*

Ruth and Boaz

Orpah did not want to leave her mother-in-law. A **tear drop** is running down her cheek in the picture on page 52. She does not know the **colors** of foreign lands, of adventure. Naomi and Ruth, on the other hand, are represented in a different **color** on page 53. It depicts that they want to explore and experience new things.

*From the **first book of Samuel**: God defeats the giant*

David Kills the Giant Goliath (16-17)

How can the **young David** defeat a **giant** like Goliath? In the picture (p. 57), the giant is so tall that only his one foot fits on the page! David is so small that **Saul's armor** is much too big for him. It is his faith in God that gives him courage and wisdom. The giant has feet of clay.

*From the **first book of Kings**: a wise king*

Wise King Solomon (3:16-28)

The "**node of Solomon**", which decorates his throne (p. 59), is a riddle that no one can solve. It represents the **wisdom** of the king. He is about to give his **judgment** to the two mothers claiming that both are the child's mother. The true mother has **light** in her heart: she cries and doesn't look away from the child. The other woman watches Solomon (p. 58).

The Queen of Sheba Visits King Solomon (10)

The Queen of Sheba is **dressed differently** from the other women portrayed in this Bible storybook, and her hair is very long (p. 60). These details indicate that she was very beautiful and came from a very far land. She knelt in front of Solomon because she acknowledged his power. Unlike the people who built the **Tower of Babel**, Solomon sees in this foreign woman, the **light** of her heart.

*From the book of **Daniel**: By believing in God, one can defeat fear, even in fire*

Three Brave Men in the Fiery Furnace (3:1-50)

As victims of the abuse of power by the king and because of **jealousy**, the three young Jews were thrown into a fiery **furnace**. But they did not burn. They overcame fear and fire by **singing praises** to the Lord.

Daniel in the Lions' Den (6:17-25)

This time, jealousy and imperial power lead **Daniel** to a den, and to the jaws of wild **lions**. But an **angel** arrived and the lions became tame like kittens. In the illustration on page 67 you can see the **friendly expressions** on the lions' faces, like in the Garden of Eden where harmony and **peace** reigned.

*From the book of **Jonah**: when the one that eats you protects you*

Jonah and the Big Fish (2)

Jonah is swallowed by a **big fish**. Just like the three young Jews that were thrown into the fire, Jonah, when he is in the fish's belly, **praises** the Lord! When he arrives in Nineveh, Jonah is alone. The people **look at him with concern**. Even the **king appears** at the window of his palace (p. 70). Jonah does not know yet that he will convert the entire city, thanks to the **words** that God will put in his mouth.

THE NEW TESTAMENT

An Angel Visits Mary

The Angel Gabriel announces

the word of God. He has in his hands a **scroll** of paper that unfolds in the divine **light**, the same one that shines on the young woman, Mary (p. 75). You can see a **dove** beside the window. It had carried the hope of Noah's **Ark** that now represents the **Holy Spirit** and is bringing to Mary a unique gift: the birth of Jesus.

Baby Jesus Is Born
In Bethlehem there was no room left for Mary and Joseph to sleep. In the picture (p. 77), the hotel owner points out a **stable**, a poor and simple (but warm and intimate) place. Jesus was born among animals, in simplicity, and He became a human like all of us.

The Wise Men Visit Baby Jesus
In the illustration, **Herod** is imprisoned in his palace, keeping everything to himself. He is incapable of giving. He only thinks about his **crown**: it is big, like his power (p. 80). The Wise Men, on the other hand, like Abraham and Ruth, go on a very long **journey**, and carry **gifts** to Jesus of gold, Frankincense and myrrh.

Joseph and Mary Find Jesus in the Temple
In the illustration, the **teachers** of the Law are represented as **symbols of wisdom**. Each one of them is standing, like a **pillar**, confident in its own power (p. 83). Jesus, however, as seen in the picture, is **sitting**, and you can see the **light** behind Him. His **eyes** are

turned to the reader, showing that His **wisdom** wants to meet with you; He wants to be your friend.

Jesus Is Baptized
In the picture (p. 84-85), open skies are shown, indicating that there is **communication between the sky and the earth**, between God and people.
  Jesus is not afraid of the water, He gets baptized like everyone else and the **light** surrounds Him (p. 85). Once again, the **dove**, the Holy Spirit, lets Him know that the Father of the skies loves Him very much; He is now ready to preach the Gospel to all.

The Twelve Disciples
Jesus finds new friends, the apostles. Jesus was walking on the beach when He found His disciples. They were busy fishing. Jesus **called** them. Why do they listen to Him? Because they trusted such a special friend. It is not important that they are **different**, or that their clothes look different: Jesus calls them by their names, He wants to know each one of them personally.

Jesus Preaches to the People
People from all over came to listen to Jesus, because the **light** of God could be seen through Him. His powerful words were words of happiness and hope. In the crowd depicted on page 92, there is a child with white and red

stripes on his tunic, and a belt around it. Remember him: you will see him again later.
  The **Word** of Jesus is so wonderful that you can compare it to a house built on a rock. In the picture on page 95, the house on the rock is illuminated with the same color as Jesus' clothes. Evil cannot destroy a house built on a rock.

Jesus Gives Food to a Big Crowd
The child wearing the tunic with the red and white stripes and belt is generous: he is holding a basket with **bread** and fish that he kindly offers to Jesus (p. 97). With just a little, everyone gets enough! Giving what you have is enough, and Jesus makes a miracle out of it! It is strange, but the **bread** has the same **color as the light** around Jesus: not only does it appease hunger, but it also appeases the desires of the heart.

Jesus Walks on Water
Peter wants to prove his courage and climbs out of the boat, but it is difficult to walk on the **waters of evil**. Peter risks drowning and he needs help to get back in the **boat**. Only with Jesus can we confront the **waters of evil**.

Jesus Teaches What Is Important
In order to love, a **big heart** is needed, like Jesus' heart (p. 101). Only the heart of the one that loves can welcome the **light**. In Jesus' heart there is

room for everyone.

The Wedding at Cana
At a wedding, the wine is the symbol of the party celebrations, but if there is no wine, there is no celebration. Mary notices that there is no more wine and she takes the initiative to find a solution: she becomes the **intermediary** between Jesus and the servants.

The Good Samaritan
To get from Jerusalem to Jericho the road goes **downhill** (p. 102). This suggests that it is not an easy route. There are thieves and one can get killed. The Good Samaritan is provident, as he takes on his journey a little **bottle of oil** and some **wine** that may help someone who is in need.

Jesus Brings Lazarus Back to Life
Martha and Mary were crying because their brother, Lazarus, was dead and buried. The two sisters differed a lot. On page 107, notice Martha's **hands** and her **apron**: she is the woman who takes care of the house. Mary's ear is visible in the picture as she liked to listen to the **word** of God. Jesus loved all the members of this family, so He prayed to God, His Father, to send light from the sky and that His friend Lazarus would be resurrected.

The Lord's Prayer
The secret of Jesus' life was His **relationship with His**

Father. That is why He is clothed in **white** (p. 108). The **light** also follows Him all the time. With His arms raised toward the sky, Jesus wants to reveal the **secret** for a holy life to His apostles, who are looking at Him in amazement.

The Prodigal Son

The illustration shows a son **without shoes**, with **clothes all patched up**, who goes back home after many years, and who has lost all his money and even his dignity (p. 110).

The **arms** of the father who kisses his son are depicted in a very specific way (p. 113): one is the arm of a man (big hand), and the other one is the arm of a woman (smaller hand). Love with the love of a mother and the love of a father: Love as God does!

Jesus and the Children

Just like in the illustration on page 83 of Jesus in the temple, here on page 115 His eyes **are turned toward the reader**. He touches us with His tender gestures. All the children look at Jesus, with smiles on their faces. The children are all **different**, each one is special. Among them you can recognize the boy with the striped tunic from the story on page 97. In this illustration Jesus is illuminated by **light**. He enlightens and points out the path of truth. The children should not be afraid of Him, but instead, they can get closer, and even kiss Him. It is truly "God among us".

Jesus Goes to Jerusalem

In ancient times, a horse was an animal of war, and the **donkey** was the animal of peace. Jesus entered Jerusalem on the back of a donkey because He is the King of peace. That is the reason why He is welcomed with songs and palm tree branches. Among the crowds in the picture (p. 117) is the child in the striped tunic, waving a branch: he has followed Jesus to Jerusalem.

Jesus' Last Supper

Just like in Cana, Jesus is also sitting at a table. One thing to notice in the picture (p. 118-119) is the same beautiful **tablecloth** and the same wine as in the illustration on page 90-91. This relates to the Last Supper and a few details should be noted: all the disciples are looking at Jesus, except Judas, the traitor. The **bread** is the same color as the loaves of bread on page 95. It is special bread.

Jesus Prays in the Garden of Gethsemane

Jesus is alone in the garden. But the **light** of the Father remains with Him (p. 122-123). It will help Him to fight **evil**. Take note of the truth of an old proverb: "Better to **light** a candle than to **curse the darkness**."

Jesus Is Arrested

Judas is a traitor; he wants Jesus to be arrested by armed soldiers and he betrays Him with a kiss. Jesus is ready, but

the apostles, **hidden** behind a tree, are **afraid**. Jesus is alone, but He will confront His destiny.

Peter Says He Doesn't Know Jesus

When the rooster crows, Peter, the **rock**, finally starts to cry and repents. He knows that he had denied knowing His Master. He **opens up his heart** (p. 126). Only the one who admits his own mistakes can have sympathy for other sinners.

Jesus and Pilate

Jesus is **chained** by men, but His **heart is free**. Pilate is **free** from men, but his heart is **chained** by power as is depicted in the picture where he is sitting in his chair (p. 129).

Jesus Carries His Cross to Golgotha

Jesus is carrying on His shoulders the weight of the cross and He is still walking: He is a true King! Why? He wears a **red coat** and a **crown made of thorns**. Instead of giving up, He is walking: it is the sign of a majesty which is not human, but divine. Jesus "reigns like a God"!

Jesus Dies and Is Buried

Jesus is crucified: the thief on His right **looks** at Him, and the other one looks away. See the illustration on page 133. It is not easy to look at Jesus on the cross, but it is important because even when He is weak and dying, your trust must be in Him. At the foot of the

cross, Mary and John try to remain close to Him during this time of great pain. In such solitude, everything seems to end when everything was in fact beginning.

Mary Magdalene Sees Jesus Is Alive

Jesus comes back to life and everything returns to a setting similar to the beginning of Creation: the atmosphere is the same as in the **Garden of Eden**. Mary Magdalene does not cry anymore, but she **kneels** in front of Jesus Christ, who has overcome death (p. 135).

The Road to Emmaus

Jesus Christ comes back to life and appears to the disciples on their way to Jerusalem. He listens to their questions all along the **journey**. He is illuminated by **light** (p. 136).

Jesus Goes Back to Heaven

The **light** of the heavenly Father that had fallen upon Mary of Nazareth is the same light as the one that follows Jesus throughout His earthly life, even in darkness. From there on, Jesus Christ is ready to go back to heaven (p. 139). This **light**, which you have seen "at the beginning of the world" is a gift for you, for everyone. The child that has given bread and fish to Jesus, and who followed Him to Jerusalem appears here again. He has a story to tell: Offer these colors and give these words to those who let themselves be guided by the **Light**.

Dear Parents,

Books are not only objects to read or to browse. They are much more than that. They are very important and fun companions to help educate your children. By following the advice below, you will learn how to use this book in a better way to teach and share with your children the priceless pleasure of reading.

- Make an effort to read to your children regularly as it creates good parent-child relationships. It stimulates their imagination and logical thinking, while expanding their vocabulary and developing their ability to express themselves.
- Explain the stories of the Bible to your children by looking at the illustrations. Refer to the explanations at the back of the book to help you explain the symbolism of the illustrations. These explanations will prove useful in teaching your children to read and interpret pictures.
- Reading books out loud and commenting on the stories (without exaggerating), articulating words correctly and increasing the reading pace where the stories require it, will encourage individual reading.
- Let your children open and close books whenever and how often they want.
- Create a space where your children can have easy access to books.
- Let them play with the books and try to invent their own games based on the stories. They can also change the ending of a story or make up an entirely new story.

Keep in mind that the recommended reading age of children differs with each one's reading experience.